SUMMARY & ANALYSIS

OF

THE SECOND MOUNTAIN

The Quest For a Moral Life

A GUIDE TO THE BOOK
BY DAVID BROOKS

NOTE: This book is a summary and analysis and is meant as a companion to, not a replacement for, the original book.

Please follow this link to purchase a copy of the original book: https://amzn.to/2MsTL9i

---

Copyright © 2019 by ZIP Reads. All rights reserved. This book or parts thereof may not be reproduced in any form, stored in any retrieval system, or transmitted in any form by any means—electronic, mechanical, photocopy, recording, or otherwise—without prior written permission of the publisher, except as provided by United States of America copyright law. This book is intended as a companion to, not a replacement for the original book. ZIP Reads is wholly responsible for this content and is not associated with the original author in any way.

TABLE OF CONTENTS

SYNOPSIS ... 8

PART I: THE TWO MOUNTAINS ... 10

CHAPTER ONE: MORAL ECOLOGIES ... 10

Key Takeaway: A society's moral ecology always moves in a specific cycle. ... 10

Key Takeaway: Hyper-individualism as a moral ecology is based on 5 core ideas. ... 10

CHAPTER TWO: THE INSTAGRAM LIFE ... 11

Key Takeaway: Many young people have fallen into an aesthetic lifestyle that leads nowhere. ... 11

CHAPTER THREE: THE INSECURE OVERACHIEVER ... 12

Key Takeaway: Overachievers appear pragmatic but are actually driven by anxiety. ... 12

Key Takeaway: Meritocracy has become the preeminent moral system. ... 13

Key Takeaway: Acedia is much more common today than ever. ... 13

CHAPTER FOUR: THE VALLEY ... 14

Key Takeaway: The valley is defined by suffering. ... 14

Key Takeaway: There are two forms of telos crisis. ... 14

Key Takeaway: Individualism has created four social crises. ... 15

CHAPTER FIVE: THE WILDERNESS ... 15

Key Takeaway: In the wilderness of life, you must embrace suffering and solitude. ... 15

Key Takeaway: Learn to listen to what life is telling you.. 16

CHAPTER SIX: HEART AND SOUL............................16

Key Takeaway: It is your soul that bears moral worth and responsibility. 16

CHAPTER SEVEN: THE COMMITTED LIFE 17

Key Takeaway: the second mountain is the antithesis of the individualistic culture. 17

Key Takeaway: Commitment means falling in love with something and then structuring it. 17

Key Takeaway: There are four major benefits of a committed life. 18

CHAPTER EIGHT: THE SECOND MOUNTAIN 18

Key Takeaway: People on the second mountain experience a shift in desires. 19

Key Takeaway: Weavers tend to be extremely relational. 20

PART II: VOCATION 21

CHAPTER NINE: WHAT VOCATION LOOKS LIKE....21

Key Takeaway: A vocation and a career are two very different things. 21

Key Takeaway: Finding your vocation can be a messy and confusing process. 21

CHAPTER 10: THE ANNUNCIATION MOMENT 22

Key Takeaway: Annunciation moments define your perspective and trajectory in life. 22

Key Takeaway: Most people are not even aware when they are having an annunciation moment. 22

CHAPTER 11: WHAT MENTORS DO 23

Key Takeaway: A good mentor is more valuable than a good book. 23

Key Takeaway: The best mentors know how to balance love with relentlessly high standards. 24

CHAPTER 12: VAMPIRE PROBLEMS 24

Key Takeaway: When making transformative decisions, intuition isn't the best solution. 25

Key Takeaway: Rational decision-making trumps intuition, but you're better off finding your daemon. 25

CHAPTER 13: MASTERY 26

Key Takeaway: There's a difference between a job and work. 26

Key Takeaway: Succeeding at a vocation requires discipline and dedication. 26

PART III: MARRIAGE 28

CHAPTER 14: THE MAXIMUM MARRIAGE 28

Key Takeaway: There are three factors that water down a maximum marriage. 28

Key Takeaway: Marriage teaches you to be less selfish. 28

CHAPTER 15: THE STAGES OF INTIMACY I 29

Key Takeaway: Initial courtship occurs in four key stages. 29

CHAPTER 16: THE STAGES OF INTIMACY II 29

Key Takeaway: After the initial combustion, someone must take a leap of faith. 29

Key Takeaway: At some point, love will turn into frustration. 30

Key Takeaway: Every relationship crisis should be followed by forgiveness. 30

CHAPTER 17: THE MARRIAGE DECISION 31

Key Takeaway: Before you get married, you need to ask yourself some tough questions. 31

Key Takeaway: When making a marriage decision, apply three important lenses. 32

CHAPTER 18: MARRIAGE: THE SCHOOL YOU BUILD TOGETHER I 32

Key Takeaway: Marriage recommitment is essential especially after the love dries up. 33

Key Takeaway: The second love is always sweeter than the first one. 33

PART IV: PHILOSOPHY AND FAITH 34

CHAPTER 19: INTELLECTUAL COMMITMENTS 34

Key Takeaway: Universities have abandoned the humanistic ideal in favor of a research ideal. 34

Key Takeaway: Universities are supposed to teach students six core intellectual virtues. 34

CHAPTER 20: RELIGIOUS COMMITMENT 35

Key Takeaway: Those who have never had spiritual experiences tend to disbelieve them. 36

CHAPTER 21: A MOST UNEXPECTED TURN OF EVENTS 36

Key Takeaway: Judaism and Christianity represent contradictory traditions. 36

Key Takeaway: The process of internal transformation is gradual. 37

CHAPTER 22: RAMPS AND WALLS 38

Key Takeaway: On the journey to find God, you will encounter different kinds of obstacles. 38

Key Takeaway: Religion also has ramps that make the spiritual journey easier. 38

PART V: COMMUNITY 40

CHAPTER 23: THE STAGES OF COMMUNITY BUILDING I 40

Key Takeaway: A community is more than just buildings and streets. 40

Key Takeaway: The social fabric of America is torn. 40

Key Takeaway: To renew a community requires selflessness and radical, innovative changes. 41

CHAPTER 24: THE STAGES OF COMMUNITY BUILDING II 41

Key Takeaway: Communal stories that define a shared history can bring people together. 41

Key Takeaway: The neighbor code is built around specific principles. 42

CHAPTER 25: CONCLUSION: THE RELATIONALIST MANIFESTO 42

Key Takeaway: Hyper-individualism is an attempt to break free from the chains of society. 43

Key Takeaway: Relationalism is about interconnectedness and social commitment. 43

EDITORIAL REVIEW 44

BACKGROUND ON AUTHOR 47

Titles by David Brooks 49

SYNOPSIS

In his book, *The Second Mountain: The Quest for a Moral Life*, David Brooks narrates the difference between two moral perspectives. The first mountain refers to the stage in life when people focus on individualistic and egotistical pursuits, e.g. career and money. The second mountain is the stage most people reach later in life. They begin to focus more on matters of the heart and soul, e.g. building communities, relationships, and finding their true calling.

The book is in five parts. Brooks starts off by describing the moral ecologies of the two mountains. He emphasizes the fact that moral values cannot be replaced by autonomy, individualism, and meritocracy. He then discusses the importance of having a vocation rather than a career, and why it's important to have a mentor to help you discover your true calling.

As the book continues, Brooks talks about the concept of marriage and the stages of intimacy in a relationship. He also delves into philosophy and faith, advocating for the need to maintain intellectual and religious commitments to ourselves and our community.

He wraps up the book by discussing how to renew fractured communities. He recommends that neighbors come together and care for one another. Communal support is the only way to avert the crises of social isolation and the tearing of the social fabric.

Ultimately, Brooks believes that every individual should live their life from a heart and soul perspective, motivated by the burning desire to serve others using their talents and passion.

PART I: THE TWO MOUNTAINS

CHAPTER ONE: MORAL ECOLOGIES

Brooks opens the book by explaining how moral ecologies have defined and continue to define society and individuals. A moral ecology is a set of beliefs and values that guides an individual or a society. They guide dressing, speech, and culture. However, moral ecologies tend to have virtues as well as failings.

Key Takeaway: A society's moral ecology always moves in a specific cycle.

Brooks claims that over time, the moral ecology of a society shifts in a particular pattern. The first phase is the 'ratchet" phase where society uses a moral ecology to solve its problems. Then comes the "hatchet" phase where a counterculture rises up and does away with the old ecology because it cannot solve new problems. As the battle between old and new rages, society ultimately chooses to adopt a new moral ecology. Thus the cycle repeats itself.

Key Takeaway: Hyper-individualism as a moral ecology is based on 5 core ideas.

According to Brooks, the culture of hyper-individualism that has become so dominant in society is built on:

The autonomous self – People want to have as much freedom as possible with little control from general society.

God within – People believe that the definitive source of authority should be the voice within.

Privatization of meaning – Everyone wants to create their personal value and morality system.

Total freedom – Individuals want to be free from institutional influence, e.g. family, religion, and culture.

Accomplishments – Individuals are measured according to status and wealth rather than a moral code.

CHAPTER TWO: THE INSTAGRAM LIFE

In a world plagued by uncertainty, the youth are searching for meaning, direction, wisdom, and a life task to devote themselves to. However, all they get from adults are empty promises of freedom, possibility, and autonomy. This leaves them stuck in limbo.

Key Takeaway: Many young people have fallen into an aesthetic lifestyle that leads nowhere.

Once people graduate from college, they begin to seek a life of adventure and experiences. Young people are told that this is a good way to create an identity and take risks. As a result, many young people drift from job to job, house to house, and adventure to adventure. Every experience is shared on social media to show others how cool their life is. But the problem with this is that it is an aesthetic lifestyle that doesn't lead to fulfillment. By the time your thirties come around, all you have are temporary experiences and an obsession with self. Though the Internet provides great freedom, it has created a generation that is unfocused, uncommitted, and lost in cheap entertainment. Brooks states that the person who graduates and seeks such a lifestyle ultimately burns and crashes, realizing that freedom without direction or commitment sucks.

CHAPTER THREE: THE INSECURE OVERACHIEVER

Key Takeaway: Overachievers appear pragmatic but are actually driven by anxiety.

Unlike those who only care about an aesthetic lifestyle, some young people are such overachievers that they treat their adult life as a competition. These overachievers are used to doing well academically, and their dream is to get hired by prestigious firms. Brooks says that though these young adults are pragmatists and good problem solvers, they are also suppressing a sense of anxiety about their future. As a result, they take jobs that they don't love and end up as unfulfilled people-pleasers.

Key Takeaway: Meritocracy has become the preeminent moral system.

According to Brooks, moral values are supposed to help you figure out who you are and what you want in life. However, the world is using meritocracy as a replacement for the moral system. Moral concepts have now been professionalized. Instead of "character" referring to moral qualities of service, love, and care, it is now used to refer to organizational traits such as discipline, grit, and productivity. Community now refers to a group of competing employees. Meritocracy creates the impression that those who are smarter and talented are worth more than everybody else. This explains why many people who attach their worth to job titles and status end up feeling like they have lost their souls.

Key Takeaway: Acedia is much more common today than ever.

After years of chasing professional opportunities and sacrificing marriage and children, many individuals end up fantasizing about living a life of purpose and passion. This is known as acedia, which means quieting of passion or a sense of under-living your life. Brooks states that this problem has been affecting men and women for centuries. A person may have a job and family but because they are an insecure overachiever, they sacrifice joy for status and wealth.

CHAPTER FOUR: THE VALLEY

Key Takeaway: The valley is defined by suffering.

Brooks describes the valley as a season of suffering and despondency, where an individual ponders the fundamental questions of life. You begin to search for the true meaning of life. Many people who reach this stage first deny the existence of a problem by pretending that life is okay. Then they attempt to double down on their previous efforts. To numb the internal suffering, they start an affair or take drugs. Finally, when all has failed, they admit to themselves that their perspective of life must change. Brooks refers to this as a telos crisis.

Key Takeaway: There are two forms of telos crisis.

Brooks defines a telos crisis as a state in which a person doesn't recognize their purpose in life. He states that a telos crisis manifests in two ways. The first is the walking form, where the individual senses that there is something missing in their life but continues to stick to the same lifestyle. The second is the sleeping form, where the individual loses all hope, shuts down, and lives a joyless and unenthusiastic life.

Key Takeaway: Individualism has created four social crises.

Loneliness – 35 percent of Americans below the age of 45 suffer from chronic loneliness, with rates of opioid addiction and suicide skyrocketing.

Distrust – Most Americans feel alienated from one another and people no longer see the benefit of sacrifice in relationships.

Crisis of meaning – More people are losing their sense of purpose, faith, and patriotism.

Tribalism – This is what happens when people try to cure individualism. They gravitate to the opposite extreme and form tribal groups.

CHAPTER FIVE: THE WILDERNESS

Key Takeaway: In the wilderness of life, you must embrace suffering and solitude.

Most people, when faced with tough life challenges, will try to address the problem and move on. However, Brooks argues that the best way to handle your wilderness moment is to go through the suffering, learn from the experience, shed your old self, and use the wisdom obtained to serve others. In the wilderness, you must spend time alone in quiet intimacy, banishing all distractions. This will give you time to reflect on past pains and failures so that you can heal.

Key Takeaway: Learn to listen to what life is telling you.

As you review your life in the wilderness, you must learn to listen to your life. Instead of living a life that has been defined for you by others, listen and learn who you are and what your destiny is. This requires patience and the ability to embrace uncertainty. You will learn to resist jumping to conclusions about life and ultimately go deeper into your persona. You will crack that hard outer shell and reveal your true heart and soul.

CHAPTER SIX: HEART AND SOUL

No matter how hard you try to drown the innate human desire, it always finds a way to rise to the surface. Brooks argues that society has prioritized reasoning brain and ignored the heart and soul. Yet it is these two parts of human consciousness that we need to transform and live fulfilled lives.

Key Takeaway: It is your soul that bears moral worth and responsibility.

Brooks believes that we all have a soul because it is a core part of your moral consciousness. Unlike other living creatures that don't bear moral responsibility for their actions, the presence of a soul means you are always accountable for your deeds. It is your soul that earns you respect, and any action that covers up another's soul should be considered obscene and immoral. Acts such as slavery, rape, and cowardice are all unethical regardless of where you go because the human soul is wired to seek righteousness at all times.

CHAPTER SEVEN: THE COMMITTED LIFE

Brooks discusses the differences between an individualistic life and the interdependence that defines the second mountain. He also explains some of the benefits of living a committed life.

Key Takeaway: the second mountain is the antithesis of the individualistic culture.

Brooks states that individualism pushes people toward personal happiness, independence, autonomy, lecturing, worldly accomplishments, self-interest, and commercialization. On the other hand, the second mountain makes people focus on meaning, moral joy, interdependence, relation, listening, moral accomplishments, loving others, generous giving, and keeping your promises.

Key Takeaway: Commitment means falling in love with something and then structuring it.

According to Brooks, there are four major life commitments—career, family, faith, and community. Though they may appear to be distinct commitments, they are actually quite similar. They all require dedication, time and energy, single focus, and audacity. The first step in every commitment is allowing your heart and soul to fall in love with a person or idea. This usually takes time because judging whether a person or idea is worth it requires patience. The next step is to totally dedicate yourself and become willing to change who you are to make the commitment work. This may mean creating some sort of legal obligation that prevents the parties from breaking their love for one another. Therefore, a commitment must ultimately involve the establishment of a structure of behavior for those times when love isn't strong enough to hold people together.

Key Takeaway: There are four major benefits of a committed life.

Identity – They give us coherence and constancy.

Purpose – Committing to one another gives life meaning.

Freedom – You are able to move freely to something greater than yourself.

Character – Commitment builds moral character as you willingly serve others sacrificially.

CHAPTER EIGHT: THE SECOND MOUNTAIN

In this chapter, Brooks discusses the role that weavers play in the community and what motivates them. He describes weavers as people who are committed to creating a network of healthy communities by building transformational relationships. Though such people can be found in all walks of life, they do share similar traits. They all choose to make a maximum commitment to something they care about in the service of others.

Key Takeaway: People on the second mountain experience a shift in desires.

When people begin to climb their second mountain, their desires and motivations tend to transform. According to Brooks, there are six levels of desire:

1. Material possessions e.g. food, cars, and houses.

2. Ego e.g. winning and being recognized for your success.

3. Intellect – Learning and understanding the world.

4. Generosity – Pleasure you get from giving to and serving others.

5. Love – Giving and receiving love.

6. Transcendence – The pleasure of living according to ideals.

Modern culture with its hyper-individualism tends to focus on the first two desires. However, the reality is that society is built on the last four desires—moral, emotional, and spiritual motivations.

Key Takeaway: Weavers tend to be extremely relational.

Brooks states that the weavers he has met are all invested in forging deep relationships with others. They do this because they have an innate desire to connect and an undying belief that deep relationships are the only way to transform the lives of people. Unlike the large institutions and systems, weavers don't just *serve* the poor and homeless. They care for people by listening and talking to them.

PART II: VOCATION

CHAPTER NINE: WHAT VOCATION LOOKS LIKE

In this chapter, Brooks analyses the life of George Orwell and uses it to explain why having a vocation is a great thing.

Key Takeaway: A vocation and a career are two very different things.

Brooks states that career involves utilizing your frontal cortex to discover your talents, gifts, and value to society. It requires formal education and professional skills that allow you to seek a job that will reap financial rewards and respect. A vocation, on the other hand, goes beyond the ego. You do not care about financial rewards or convenience. You are driven by a deeper part of your nature that seeks to right some injustice, even if the costs outweigh the benefits. A vocation is a calling that may appear irrational because it forces an individual to step away from the herd and walk an unknown path.

Key Takeaway: Finding your vocation can be a messy and confusing process.

Many people buy into the idea that finding your calling is easy. But the truth is that discovering what you are called to do can be quite complex. However, if you look at the lives of great individuals in history, you will discover that they actually noticed their gift at an early age. But they either chose to ignore or simply forgot about it. It is only after years of wandering in confusion, trying to find something that fits, that they ultimately rediscover what they are supposed to do with their life.

CHAPTER 10: THE ANNUNCIATION MOMENT

Key Takeaway: Annunciation moments define your perspective and trajectory in life.

Brooks defines an annunciation moment as the moment when you discover or realize something that arouses your interest. This desire then becomes the guiding compass that directs you as you encounter both challenges and delights. This passionate moment can be an experience or period in life when you lose something you held dear. For example, a person born into poverty may discover a passion for business and eventually become a billionaire. It can be a child who, forced to deal with his parents' divorce, discovers a love for nature. Annunciation moments can be quite aesthetic and often strike you when you least expect it. You suddenly experience an unexplainable beauty that goes on to define your future.

Key Takeaway: Most people are not even aware when they are having an annunciation moment.

One of the best ways to discover your purpose is to look to your past. Brooks quotes Nietzsche who stated that you have to look into your past, highlight those moments when you were most fulfilled, arrange them in a row, and find the line that connects them all. This is how you will discover a law that defines your very self. However, this is challenging for many people because they rarely realize when they are having an annunciation moment. In a world filled with so many distractions, people often fail to discern those precious moments that point to their true purpose. It is only in hindsight that many individuals realize the actual moment in which they began walking toward their destiny.

CHAPTER 11: WHAT MENTORS DO

Key Takeaway: A good mentor is more valuable than a good book.

When you acquire book knowledge, you are absorbing a bunch of formulas and rules through deliberate learning. Theoretical knowledge seeks to offer you the principles of a subject or activity. However, when you have a mentor, you are gaining practical knowledge that can only be imparted. A mentor imparts in you the touch, feel, or taste necessary to excel at an activity. Instead of thinking more, a mentor shows you how to think less by practicing something until your intuition takes over. For example, you learn how to think like a biologist instead of merely earning the principles of biology.

Key Takeaway: The best mentors know how to balance love with relentlessly high standards.

Brooks claims that most young people are seeking intensity of purpose rather than happiness. This is because every individual wants to pursue a worthy mission regardless of the hardship it entails. At the core, we all desire a calling that entails sacrifice and dedication. That is why a person is more likely to remember the mentor who pushed them to their limit rather than the one who was always easy on them. A good mentor will expect you to take things seriously even as they offer their love and support. They will humble you, show you how to handle mistakes, encourage your self-confidence, and teach you how to embrace the suffering of life. Finally, a good mentor will always cut you off when it's time to let you go.

CHAPTER 12: VAMPIRE PROBLEMS

Brooks describes a vampire problem as a problem that requires you to make a transformative choice in your life. This can be the decision to get married, have kids, move to a new country, or change careers. Though all choices involve uncertainty, transformative decisions are defined by the fact that you have no idea the kind of person you will become after the transformation.

Key Takeaway: When making transformative decisions, intuition isn't the best solution.

Though some claim that the best way to make big decisions is to rely on gut feeling, Brooks argues that depending on intuition is unwise. Intuition is unstable and the feeling is usually fleeting. Intuition can also lead you astray, which is why the person you've been in love with for months can suddenly seem to be a disaster once you marry them. Intuition may be reliable when making decisions in areas you already have experience in. But since transformational choices are often unknown territory, intuition won't help you.

Key Takeaway: Rational decision-making trumps intuition, but you're better off finding your daemon.

In the present culture, rationality is touted as the best way to make a decision. Just sit down with pen and paper and weigh the pros and cons. This is quite useful because there are predetermined frameworks that anyone can use, regardless of the type of problem. But as foolproof as it seems, logic is insufficient when making major commitment decisions. Logic cannot help you answer a question about your moral purpose in life. The best option is to discover the long-term motivations of your heart and soul. This is referred to as your daemon—a manic obsession that refuses to let you go. Your daemon defines your innate desires and the wellspring of your energy. This is how to find your vocation.

CHAPTER 13: MASTERY

In this chapter, Brooks explains the concept of mastering your vocation. A vocation is not merely a job. It requires a specific set of traits that must be nurtured over time. In most cases, a vocation gets easier because you are making the same decisions over and over again until you get better at a task.

Key Takeaway: There's a difference between a job and work.

Brooks distinguishes a job and work. He defines a job as a means of earning income to survive while work is a way of fulfilling a responsibility. Work is an activity that you improve at over time, touches the lives of others, and satisfies your soul's desire for righteousness. Your real work in life will always show itself regardless of the different jobs that you do.

Key Takeaway: Succeeding at a vocation requires discipline and dedication.

Just because you have found your vocation and are no longer living in uncertainty doesn't mean the hard work is over. No matter how passionate you are, you still have to develop the discipline and dedication to continuously engage in your work. Without deliberate practice, your brain stores the new knowledge in your subconscious and automatizes the process. If you allow this to happen, you will never achieve mastery of your work. You have to keep practicing and create a structure around your work routine. Structured self-discipline through the use of rituals will help you maintain focus on your work.

PART III: MARRIAGE

CHAPTER 14: THE MAXIMUM MARRIAGE

Key Takeaway: There are three factors that water down a maximum marriage.

Brooks defines a maximum marriage as one where two people are so deeply committed to the union that they become one being. However, the assault on this kind of marriage comes in three forms:

1. A safety-first attitude – Divorce is so common that many people never fully commit.

2. Embracing a compassionate marriage – The couple just goes along to get along.

3. Culture of individualism – People focus on their own needs instead of on the marriage.

Key Takeaway: Marriage teaches you to be less selfish.

According to Brooks, marriage is a lesson in moral education. Each person goes into the marriage believing that their spouse is perfect. But later on, they discover that the other person has many flaws. You may think that your partner's selfishness is the major problem in the marriage, and the feeling may be mutual. However, to build a great marriage, each party must acknowledge their own selfishness and work toward fixing their own flaws first before pointing a finger at the other person's weaknesses.

CHAPTER 15: THE STAGES OF INTIMACY I

Key Takeaway: Initial courtship occurs in four key stages.

Brooks states that in the initial phase of courtship, a couple will share four stages of intimacy. These are:

The Glance – Two people see each other for the first time and a flame is lit.

Curiosity – You become absorbed in the other person and are constantly thinking about them.

Dialogue – You go out on dates, talk, share, and flirt.

Opening the gates – You begin to talk deeply about life, past relationships, etc.

CHAPTER 16: THE STAGES OF INTIMACY II

Key Takeaway: After the initial combustion, someone must take a leap of faith.

Part of the journey of intimacy requires that one person takes a leap. At this point, you have to ask yourself whether you can ever live without the other person. Every decision you make is now a "We" rather than an "I" decision. You give each other titles such as boyfriend or girlfriend. The relationship is now more about unselfish actions instead of just warm feelings.

Key Takeaway: At some point, love will turn into frustration.

Crisis is also another phase of intimacy. There is always a period in time when a couple will fight over something. The fight may be due to selfishness or confusion over roles. But oftentimes the fight can arise due to a central disagreement that is based on deep moral or philosophical differences. The problem is that the most superficial disagreements can also be the most painful.

Key Takeaway: Every relationship crisis should be followed by forgiveness.

Brooks claims that forgiveness isn't a simple process of mushy absolution. For it to be genuine, it must be rigorous and balanced with mercy, compassion, and accountability. The person who has been wronged must be strong enough to set aside their resentment, approach the offender, and create an opportunity for confession. The offender must then be honest enough to confess their sin and await judgment. Though it may take a while for trust to be regained, the suffering that both individuals go through ultimately strengthens the relationship.

CHAPTER 17: THE MARRIAGE DECISION

Brooks says that making the jump from courtship to marriage usually involves some tension. Am I really making the right decision? The best way to answer this question is to appraise the relationship from a rational perspective. Love and passion may hold the marriage together initially but these emotions are insufficient. Statistics show that 40 percent of American marriages end up in divorce, with seven percent staying together despite being unhappy. Society has also failed to teach couples how to make marriage decisions and instead distracts them with unimportant choices.

Key Takeaway: Before you get married, you need to ask yourself some tough questions.

Many people tend to appraise their partner when deciding whether to get married or not. However, Brook argues that you are better off appraising yourself by asking the following questions:

- Can I really do this?

- Do I like myself when I am around them?

- Does my partner fill my core issue?

- Would I enjoy talking with them for the rest of my life?

Key Takeaway: When making a marriage decision, apply three important lenses.

Psychological lens – Evaluate the other person's personality traits. Ensure they are open, conscientious, and agreeable. Also consider their upbringing, relationship with parents, and attachment style.

Emotional lens – What kind of love do you share? Is it friendship (Philia), passion (Eros), or selfless giving (Agape)? You should have all three.

Moral lens – Does your partner have a character of honesty, integrity, and good judgment? Think of the traits you would want to pass to your children.

CHAPTER 18: MARRIAGE: THE SCHOOL YOU BUILD TOGETHER I

In this chapter, Brooks explains how marriage is a lifelong education that a couple must go through together. The couple gets to know and understand each other better through quality communication. But after each crisis, they are forced to recommit to each other. Ultimately, the couple reaches the phase known as the second love, where they both become selfless.

Key Takeaway: Marriage recommitment is essential especially after the love dries up.

According to Brooks, there are two periods that symbolize a crisis in marriage. The first is the birth of children and the second is the mid-life crisis. When the children are born, it's easy to ignore the difficulties in the relationship by channeling your love to the children. When the middle age crisis arises, the tendency is to view your spouse as the biggest problem in your life. Some people choose to spend more time with friends or at work than with their spouse. When these crises arise, it is important to educate yourself on the art of recommitment. You must dig deeper into that well of love, openly confess your own mistakes, and deliberately spend more time together to heal the marriage.

Key Takeaway: The second love is always sweeter than the first one.

When a couple gets married, everything is a passionate joy. But after years of fighting and forgiving each other, they enter a phase that is more about enduring rather than passion. Brooks refers to this as second-mountain love. At this point, the couple has overcome the suffering that would have torn them apart and have taken comfort in the fact that they will stay with each other for the rest of their lives. The love they share is more selfless and giving that it has ever been.

PART IV: PHILOSOPHY AND FAITH

CHAPTER 19: INTELLECTUAL COMMITMENTS

Key Takeaway: Universities have abandoned the humanistic ideal in favor of a research ideal.

Centuries ago, universities were built to shape the characters and souls of students. This humanistic ideal was the main purpose of education, and as a result, students graduated with a high level of ethics, morality, and excellence. Today, however, universities have largely abandoned this and now focus on a research ideal. They place more emphasis on accumulating specialized knowledge in smaller fields. Students no longer learn how to look at life as a whole and people have consequently ignored the development of the soul. Brooks states that universities have become rich in information but poor in meaning.

Key Takeaway: Universities are supposed to teach students six core intellectual virtues.

Brooks reminisces about his college days at the University of Chicago. He claims that his professors taught students six major intellectual virtues that have withstood the test of time:

1. How to be a true scholar, i.e. a reader, thinker, and agitator.

2. Introduction of diverse moral ecologies such as Agnosticism, Christianity, Buddhism, African animism, etc.

3. How to see reality devoid of fear, pride, or insecurity.

4. Intellectual courage to stand up for the truth rather than being popular.

5. Emotional knowledge necessary to respond in specific situations.

6. A longing to learn and love new things, especially higher ideals and experiences.

CHAPTER 20: RELIGIOUS COMMITMENT

Brooks discusses some of the mystical experiences that various historical figures have gone through. Most of these experiences have been either outside in a natural setting or in prison. It seems as if when an individual is stripped of all the trappings of the material world, they begin to transcend to higher levels of reality. At times such as these, when you merge with your spiritual self, you discover that life is more than just a material reality. It is spiritual reality that drives our lives.

Key Takeaway: Those who have never had spiritual experiences tend to disbelieve them.

Despite the fact that many people have gone through some kind of spiritual experience that seems mystical and unexplainable, some still deny these spiritual realities. According to Brooks, this makes sense because you cannot base your life around something that you are not certain about. Those who disbelieve tend to rationalize spirituality as hallucinations or an altered state caused by the stress of brain chemicals. However, those who have gone through spiritual moments understand that everything around us is connected, and religion is simply a way of making sense of these moments.

CHAPTER 21: A MOST UNEXPECTED TURN OF EVENTS

In this chapter, Brooks explores his Jewish roots and how his life and those of his ancestors mimic that of the Biblical story of Exodus. He also traces his family history and childhood to show how he came to embrace Christianity in order to survive in New York. Brooks describes his declining faith in adulthood and how his divorce changed his perspective on the importance of religion.

Key Takeaway: Judaism and Christianity represent contradictory traditions.

Brooks describes himself as an amphibian because, though born Jewish, he also believes in Christ as the Messiah. He states that Judaism and Christianity represent different paths of life. For example, Judaism focuses more on peoplehood than faith. Especially after the events of the Holocaust, Jews place great emphasis on hard work, discipline, and worldly accomplishments. If you want to succeed, you must work to save yourself. Yet the story of Christ is not one based on worldly achievements and personal effort. Christians believe that the poor and downtrodden are more righteous, and salvation comes via faith in a savior rather than your own works. This dualism is what defines his life.

Key Takeaway: The process of internal transformation is gradual.

Brooks describes his rollercoaster journey from Judaism to Christianity and on to a decline in faith in his adulthood. But after going through a divorce and losing his sense of purpose, he ultimately discovers that faith is a means of overcoming suffering. Persistence in faith is what helps you overcome the doubt and anxiety around you, even when believers of a certain faith behave immorally. This process happens so slowly that you never realize just how much your faith has grown over time. You ultimately realize just how connected everyone is, and life becomes awesome and wondrous.

CHAPTER 22: RAMPS AND WALLS

Christianity is based on the notion that you must surrender your will to God. However, Brooks argues that God does not expect us to surrender our will entirely. Instead, He wants us to train and transform our will to align with His. Instead of expecting God to give you orders every day, learn to merge your will to the will of God. Once you know what God wants, you simply go along with His flow.

Key Takeaway: On the journey to find God, you will encounter different kinds of obstacles.

As he began his religious journey, Brooks discovered that fellow Christians can erect walls to make the process more difficult. He argues that the siege mentality is a wall that Christians use to separate themselves from secular society. Another wall is bad listening, where religious people use off-the-shelf statements instead of actually listening and answering people's questions. There is also the wall of intellectual mediocrity, where Christians refuse to challenge each other's beliefs just because they feel like they have to be nice to one another.

Key Takeaway: Religion also has ramps that make the spiritual journey easier.

Brooks notes that apart from walls, there are also six ramps in religion. These are rituals, overt faith, prayer, spiritual consciousness, the language of good and evil, and the audacity of belief. All these elements contribute to an individual's ability to worship God and form a community with other believers.

PART V: COMMUNITY

CHAPTER 23: THE STAGES OF COMMUNITY BUILDING I

Key Takeaway: A community is more than just buildings and streets.

A real community is made up of a system of relationships that is personal and organic. People willingly come together to help each other out during tough times, and one person's private life is everyone's business. Kids belong to everyone, and any misbehavior is dealt with communally. Though social pressure can often be too much, the people genuinely love and care for one another.

Key Takeaway: The social fabric of America is torn.

There was a time when neighbors would dash out of their houses in their pajamas to help search for a missing child. In some countries, this is still the case. But in modern, affluent America, the social fabric is fragmented and people live in extreme isolation. Some of the manifestations of this social isolation include the suicide epidemic, mass shootings, shorter life expectancies, and an increase in mental health issues. A society that is so radically hyper-individualized means everyone focuses on their own business, thus few people genuinely care about each other's personal life.

Key Takeaway: To renew a community requires selflessness and radical, innovative changes.

Brooks believes that the first step to community renewal is to put the community above the self. One person must commit themselves to bring people together in spite of the sacrifices they will have to make. Then you have to restructure the different systems in the entire neighborhood rather than focusing on helping one individual at a time. This can be achieved by leveraging the power of technology and creating social organizations.

CHAPTER 24: THE STAGES OF COMMUNITY BUILDING II

Key Takeaway: Communal stories that define a shared history can bring people together.

Some places like Wilkesboro, North Carolina are not doing well economically. However, Brooks states that the town still maintains a strong Appalachian identity that everyone is proud of. The people are intensely loyal to one another and will defend each other in the face of criticism by outsiders. The reason for this is that the town shares a communal story of building things from scratch. It is this story that is being retold, and as a result, people are starting to take pride in their town again. The community is now buzzing with new coffee shops, galleries, and even music festivals.

Key Takeaway: The neighbor code is built around specific principles.

Brooks argues that once a community has congregated around a story, action must be taken as a group. This code of the neighbor is based on certain principles. The citizens must realize that they have the power to change their own neighborhoods instead of waiting for their elected leaders to do something. Neighbors must invite and talk to each other. People must practice radical hospitality whenever one of their own is in need. It is also important to take care of the weakest elements in the neighborhood, that is, the young, poor, and disabled.

CHAPTER 25: CONCLUSION: THE RELATIONALIST MANIFESTO

In this final chapter, Brooks weaves together and summarizes the concepts of the first and second mountain. He contrasts the two different viewpoints—an individualistic society versus a relationist worldview—and creates a manifesto to guide society toward the second option. He argues that if society does not become more relational, people will revert to their tribal instincts and the world will experience greater conflict. A healthy society is one where individuals have found meaning and purpose in caring for one another and committing to their communities.

Key Takeaway: Hyper-individualism is an attempt to break free from the chains of society.

Hyper-individualism is based on the idea that life is a one-man journey. There are times when societal pressure can be so great that individuals sense a need to express their uniqueness. Unfortunately, this desire can be taken too far, thus creating a society of consumerism, social isolation, breakdown of the family, and conditional love.

Key Takeaway: Relationalism is about interconnectedness and social commitment.

According to Brooks, society must embrace a moral revolution if relationalism is to become the norm. We must accept that life is nourished by relationships, not individual desires. Instead of everyone being self-sufficient, every individual becomes a node within a network that is built on emotional and spiritual commitments to one another. You have to surrender and lose yourself to find yourself.

EDITORIAL REVIEW

In *The Second Mountain: The Quest For a Moral life,* Robert Brooks argues the case for a more moral and relational society. He believes that many of us focus too much on our ego and careers (the first mountain) in the early stages of life. It is only decades later, after chasing temporal selfish pleasures, that we recognize our lack of fulfillment. It is only then that we begin to seek a calling that stirs in our heart and soul. This is the beginning of the journey up the second mountain.

But why is it that today's society is so individualistic? Brooks says that back in the 1950s, life was too stifling and rigid as society expected everyone to act the same way. This forced the prevailing generation to rebel against conformity and gravitate toward extreme individualism. But decades later, people are realizing that hyper-individualism is just as bad as extreme conformity. This is evident in the way that most people today go through life with no sense of purpose or meaning.

When you are climbing that first mountain, all you care about is your autonomy and freedom. This is where many people end up making the wrong marriage and career decisions which ultimately lead to misery. After reaching the top of that first mountain, you descend into the valley. This is where your mid-life crisis happens. The job sucks and the money and fame no longer have any appeal. Most people succumb to depression while others self-medicate using drugs, alcohol, and illicit sex. Though the valley is a place of anguish, it can also be the most precious season because it serves to wake you up to the possibility of a better life. It exposes your vanity and humbles you.

To climb the second mountain, you must first find your heart and soul through solitude and quiet reflection. If you listen to what your soul is telling you, you will realize that your ego is your enemy. Therefore, for transformation to occur, your ego must die. Unfortunately, the ego is only killed by a fall, whether it's an illness, job loss, death, etc. Your old desires are suddenly shed and you realize that fulfillment is attached to a vocation that you use to serve others.

For some reason, Brooks believes that religion is better than spirituality. He sees spirituality as a "transcendental emotion that merely soothes" but religion as a deeper communal obligation. Many would disagree considering how religion divides people in today's world.

There is also a chapter where Brooks touts the benefits of marriage and how it makes you unselfish and more moral. This is strange advice considering that he divorced his wife and married his secretary! However, he does a good job of highlighting the key stages that define relationship intimacy and marriage. He seems to have spent time after his divorce ruminating on how to forge a strong union.

This is a great book that highlights the contrast between a hyper-individualistic society and one that is built on relationships. For the world to change for the better, we must build moral and spiritual communities where people actually care for each other's wellbeing. The more relational we are, the happier we become.

BACKGROUND ON AUTHOR

David Brooks is an American political and cultural commentator, author, and radio host. He has authored five books and written numerous op-eds for various major newspapers in America.

He was born in Toronto, Canada on August 11, 1961. His family later moved to Lower Manhattan where his father worked as an English professor at New York University and his mother studies history at Columbia. Though Jewish, he attended an Episcopalian primary school and in 1979, he graduated from Radnor High School. He earned a history degree from the University of Chicago in 1983.

After graduating, he worked as a police reporter in Chicago. He later went on to work for the *National Review, Washington Times, The Wall Street Journal, Weekly Standard,* and *The New York Times.* He has worked in various capacities as a movie review critic, book reviewer, editor, and op-ed columnist.

He published his first book in the year 2000, earning himself a name as a conservative culture critic. Though his second book was not as well received, his third book, published in 2011, was ranked number 3 on the *Publisher's Weekly* bestselling list of nonfiction works.

Brooks married his first wife, Sarah, in 1986 but were divorced in 2014. They have three kids, Joshua, Naomi, and Aaron. Brooks married his second wife, Anne Snyder, in 2017.

TITLES BY DAVID BROOKS

The Second Mountain: The Quest for a Moral Life (2019)

The Road To Character (2015)

The Social Animal: The Hidden Sources of Love, Character and Achievement (2011)

On Paradise Drive: How We Live Now (And Always Have) in the Future Tense (2004)

Bobos in Paradise: The New Upper Class and How They Got There (2000)

OF BOOK SUMMARY

ed this ZIP Reads publication, we
ge you to purchase a copy of <u>the original book.</u>

d also love an honest review on Amazon.com!

Want **FREE** book summaries delivered weekly? Sign up for our email list and get notified of all our new releases, free promos, and $0.99 deals!

No spam, just books.

Sign up at <u>www.zipreads.co</u>

Made in the USA
Coppell, TX
09 December 2020